AIR FRYER COOKBOOK FOR BEGINNERS

365 Quick and Easy, Affordable, and Budget-friendly Air Fryer Recipes for Beginners | Fry, Bake, Grill, Roast and Seafood Most Wanted Family Meals
New Edition

-By Olivia Kaur

TABLE OF CONETENTS

INTRODUCTION

What exactly is an air fryer?

In the kitchen, an air fryer is used similarly to an oven. People prepare and roast various items on top of the machine using specialized heating elements. Along with these heating components, there is a big fan that promotes quicker convection and more efficient cooking. This results in delightfully crispy and fresh food.

Philips Electronics Company patented the air fryer some time ago. The patent describes a kitchen tool that cooks food with hot air and little or no oil instead of deep frying.

The major reason people prefer air fryers to other ways of cooking are that they use much less oil than deep frying.

They're also considerably faster at cooking large amounts of food than an oven, owing to the close proximity of the heating components to the materials being cooked and the strong fan aiding the cooking process. You can obtain a healthy supper in less time, which is enough to make anybody fall in love with the fantastic air fryer.

We'll go into the several advantages of utilizing an air fryer over other cooking methods later in this book. First, we'll go through the fundamental distinctions between an air fryer and a deep fryer, since many people get them mixed up.

What's the difference between an air fryer and a deep fryer?

Unlike deep fryers, which cook your food in a vast volume of heated oil, air fryers use much less oil. Instead, they bake the ingredients until they are thoroughly done, using heating elements and a huge fan.

Deep fryers heat the oil to a certain temperature, allowing you to cook your food fast and conveniently. As a result, you must wait for the machine to heat up before adding your ingredients, which might add substantial time to your cooking process.

Air fryers do not need to be preheated before you begin cooking.

You may immediately begin by adding your components. Furthermore, you will not need to add oil to your air fryer. As a result, your meal will not necessarily be fried. It is going to be cooked.

If you use an air fryer, you won't get the same batter coating that you would with a deep fryer. If you wish to use a batter and cook it in an air fryer, spray cooking oil over the meal before putting it in the machine. This oil allows the food to absorb the oil and make a tasty, crispy batter.

What Can You Make With an Air Fryer?

As you go through this book, you will see the wide range of meals and snacks that you may prepare using an air fryer. Whether you want to cook fresh meats, seafood, and veggies or thaw and cook frozen dishes, your reliable air fryer can handle it all.

Most meats may take a bit of extra oil to cook correctly, but it will still be significantly less than the quantity of oil used in a deep fryer. If the meat has been marinated in a lot of sauce, you may not need to add any oil, but this will be mentioned in the recipe. Similarly, if you want your vegetables to be especially crispy, cover them quickly with oil. When cooking in an air fryer, it is advised that you use vegetable oil rather than butter. Because of its greater smoke point, oil warms up significantly faster than butter. It can also endure the air fryer's high temperatures. All of the recipes in this book call for olive oil, although practically any plant-based oil should work in your machine.

How Do Air Fryer Machines Work?

Air fryers operate using a heating mechanism at the top of the machine and a huge fan located lower down or along the sides of the machine. The mesh basket in the air fryer's interior chamber is where you put your ingredients.

When you turn on the air fryer, the components begin to heat up quickly. The huge fan will start spinning to circulate the heated air around the inside. This quick circulation will warm your meal, leaving it golden and crisp.

Who Can Make Use of an Air Fryer?

The beauty of air fryers is that they can be used by anybody. They're straightforward and easy to use, and they're a cheap kitchen tool. They don't take up much room in your kitchen, but they may provide you with a healthy cooking technique that allows you to produce any meal you choose.

Perhaps you're new to cooking and are searching for a simple method to make your favorites meals. Perhaps you're a skilled chef looking for a more efficient way to prepare complicated dishes at home. Or maybe you fall somewhere in the middle and consider yourself an average chef.

An air fryer will be suitable for you regardless of where you lie on the culinary spectrum! Even if you're unsure how to use your air fryer at first, you'll get more familiar with the equipment with time. You'll be preparing wonderful foods with ease before you realize it.

How Do You Make Use of an Air Fryer?

Most air fryers come with an instruction booklet that you may refer to while cooking, but here are some basic suggestions to get you started.

- Place your ingredients in the air fryer's mesh basket. The quantity of food you use will need to be adjusted depending on the size of your air fryer. Avoid overfilling the air fryer as this may interfere with the cooking process.
- If using oil, add a little more. To coat the ingredients in the oil, toss them around
- Set the time and temperature. Most air fryers feature pre-set periods and temperatures, making it very easy to cook your food for the appropriate length of time. Usually, the time is between 5 and 30 minutes, and the temperature is between 180 and 250 degrees Celsius.
- Relax and let the air fryer do its thing. You may leave the air fryer to cook your foods after you've prepared them and selected the time and temperature.
- When your meal is done, let the air fryer cool before wiping it clean.

Which Air Fryer Is the Best?

There are various types of air fryers on the market. They all have different settings and features, so the best one for you will depend on your needs and preferences.
If you don't know which one to purchase, we've produced a brief list of some of the greatest selections.

- ✓ Air Fryer Philips Avance Turbo-Star
- ✓ Air Fryer Ninja Foodi MAX 14-in-1 SmartLid
- ✓ Air Fryer by Black and Decker
- ✓ Air Fryer Tower TM17023
- ✓ The Air Fryer PowerXL Vortex
- ✓ The COSORI Air Fryer COSORI Air Fryer

Examine each choice and choose the one that best meets your requirements. Remember to include it in the cost of each one, since prices may vary greatly across brands.

What Are the Benefits of an Air Fryer?

There are several benefits to having an air fryer and utilizing it to prepare meals and snacks. Here are some of the primary advantages.

There is no need for preheating

When utilizing an air fryer, you won't have to wait for the components to warm up, nor will you have to wait for significant amounts of oil to heat up before adding your ingredients (since you don't actually need any oil)!
Your cooking procedure will be considerably faster and easier since there will be no preheating. If you're searching for a method to simplify your cooking process and save time in the kitchen, an air fryer might be the ideal solution.

They cook your food quickly and efficiently

Air fryers are particularly effective at frying your food due to the powerful heating components and the huge fan that circulates the hot air within the cooking basket. They also uniformly cook your food, so you can be confident that all of your meat and fish items are properly cooked all the way through.
The quick frying method gives your food a delicious, crispy crust that you can only get with the great air fryer.

There is no need to use a lot of oil

Many people like the crunchy coating that a deep fryer provides on their meals. However, deep fryers need a large amount of oil to be supplied in order for your food to be adequately cooked.

When using an air fryer, you don't need to use any oil at all with most items and just a little amount when utilizing meats and veggies. This results in a healthier, less fatty, yet equally tasty dinner.

If you are trying to lose weight by eating less saturated fat or fewer calories, replacing your deep fryer with an air fryer can help you.

They are simple and quick to clean. Most air fryers include pre-programmed settings that allow you to easily pick a frying time and temperature. All you have to do is add your components and choose the appropriate setting for your requirements.
This makes air fryers simple to operate for everyone, even those who have never worked in a kitchen before. It also makes these useful kitchen devices much easier to use and organize while you're in the thick of cooking.

As soon as your meal is done, use a towel and spray to rapidly clean the exterior of the machine. After the machine has cooled down, use the same towel to wipe the inside component. The mesh basket is detachable and dishwasher safe.

They may be used to prepare a wide range of foods.

When it comes to the enormous number of various air fryer recipes available for you to follow, this recipe book is merely a drop in the bucket. There is no lack of air fryer compatible recipes to peruse online or in cookbooks like this one if you're searching for some new breakfast ideas, lunchtime delights, or nighttime dinners to prepare.
Those of you who like variety in your meals will be pleased with the wide variety of foods that the air fryer can generate.
Every night, you will have the chance to sample a fresh and unique cuisine.

They occupy very little room in your kitchen.

Air fryers are small and convenient. They take up very little space in your kitchen, making them excellent for folks with tiny kitchens. They are also easy to store in your cabinets because they are small and easy to carry.
Most of them are sleek black or silver in color, so they look wonderful on your kitchen countertop. And, since they're little, they won't get in the way of your cooking.

What Are the Cons of Using an Air Fryer?

It's only fair that we highlight some of the drawbacks of utilizing an air fryer. Nonetheless, we feel that the benefits far exceed the downsides!
The following are the two primary downsides of utilizing an air fryer:

- Because of the quick heating of the components in the machine, there is an increased danger of your food burning.
- Since no oil is utilized, you may be missing out on vital monounsaturated and polyunsaturated fats. Of course, you may obtain your fats from other sources, but plant-based oils are one of the best ways to boost your omega-3 and omega-6 fatty acid consumption.

To avoid these issues, keep an eye on your food while it cooks in the air fryer. If it seems to be on the verge of burning, reduce the heat slightly.
You might improve your healthy fat intake by adding a little dab of oil to your air fryer. Alternatively, you might boost your consumption of the following foods, which are high in unsaturated fats:

- Avocados
- Seeds and nuts.
- Fish with fat.
- Lentils and pulses
- Bea

AIR FRYER RECIPES

Now that we've covered the fundamentals of what an air fryer is, how it works, and what it can do for you, it's time to put everything into action. The rest of this book is full of healthy, easy-to-make recipes that all use an air fryer as the main method of cooking.

Are you searching for a fun way to change up your morning routine and try something other than cereal and toast? Do you need some ideas to make your lunchtime more pleasurable and fascinating every day? Are you looking for delectable family-friendly meals that both you and your children will enjoy?

If any of the above describes you, you'll want to keep reading!

We've compiled a list of fantastic recipes for every meal of the day, as well as several sides, desserts, and snacks.

Let's get started with the cookbook's recipes!

BREAKFAST RECIPES

Apple and Cinnamon Fritters in the Air Fryer

- This recipe serves 4 people.
- Preparation time: 20 minutes
- 5 minutes of cooking time.

Nutritional data per serving: 102 calories, 17 grams of carbohydrates, 4 grams of protein, and 4 grams of fat.

Ingredients:

- Two apples, green
- Plain flour (200 g/7 oz)
- 2 tablespoons of brown sugar.
- 1 tsp. baking powder
- 1/2 teaspoon of salt.
- 1 teaspoon ground cinnamon
- 1 teaspoon nutmeg, ground
- 2 tablespoons of butter.
- ONE EGG
- Milk (100 mL)

Method:

1. Peel and chop the apples into tiny bits. Set it aside in a mixing dish.
2. In a large mixing bowl, combine the plain flour, brown sugar, baking powder, salt, powdered cinnamon, and ground nutmeg.
3. Melt the butter in a heatproof bowl in the microwave for 30 seconds.
4. Combine the egg and butter by whisking them together. Mix in the milk well.
5. Fold the wet ingredients into the dry mixture until it forms soft dough.
6. Wrap the dough in tin foil and chill it in the refrigerator for 10 minutes.
7. Meanwhile, preheat the air fryer to 180 degrees Celsius (350 degrees Fahrenheit) and line the basket with parchment paper.
8. Take the dough out of the fridge and shape it into small fritters with a spoon. Cook the fritters in the air fryer for 5–6 minutes, or until crispy.

Breakfast Cups with Spinach and Eggs from the Air Fryer

- This recipe serves 4 people.
- Preparation time: 5 minutes
- Time to cook: 10 minutes.

Nutritional data per serving: 176 calories, 10 grams of carbohydrates, 8 grams of protein, and 7 grams of fat.

Ingredients:

- Eight eggs
- 100 g fresh spinach (3.5 oz.)
- 50 g grated cheddar cheese (1.8 oz)
- 1 teaspoon ground black pepper

Method:

1. Preheat your air fryer to 200 °C (400 °F) and line or butter an 8-cup muffin tray.
2. Press the spinach leaves gently into the bottom of each muffin cup.
3. Place 2 eggs in each cup on top of the spinach, and sprinkle with shredded cheddar cheese and black pepper.
4. Place the muffins in the air fryer and cook for 10 minutes, or until the eggs are set.
5. 5. Serve while still hot for breakfast.

Breakfast Burritos in the Air Fryer

- This recipe serves 4 people.
- Preparation time: 20 minutes
- Time to cook: 20 minutes.

Nutritional data per serving: 450 calories, 31 grams of carbohydrates, 10 grams of protein, and 12 grams of fat.

Ingredients:

- 1 medium white potato
- 2 tablespoons of olive oil.
- 1 teaspoon sea salt
- 1 teaspoon ground black pepper
- 8 uncooked sausages.
- 4 flour tortillas (whole meal).
- Four eggs
- Milk (200 mL)
- 100 g (3.5 oz) grated cheddar

Method:

1. Preheat your air fryer to 200° Celsius (400° Fahrenheit) and line the bottom of the basket with parchment paper.
2. Peel the potato and cut it into small pieces. Toss with 1 tablespoon of olive oil and a dash of salt and pepper in a mixing dish.
3. Cook the potato cubes for 7-8 minutes in the air fryer. From the oven and drain it on paper towels.
4. In a medium pan, heat 1 tablespoon of olive oil and add the sausages. Cook for 5 minutes, or until the edges are slightly browned. Remove and put aside the sausages. Allow the sausage juices to remain in the pan.
5. In a mixing bowl, whisk together the eggs and milk, then pour into the heated skillet. Cook the eggs, scrambling them with a fork or spoon. After removing from the skillet, set aside.
6. In a large mixing bowl, combine the potatoes, sausages, scrambled eggs, and cheddar cheese.
7. Spread the mixture equally on four whole-grain wheat tortillas and shape them into burritos. Use a toothpick to hold them together.
8. Cook the burritos in a hot air fryer for 7-8 minutes, flipping halfway through.
9. Serve this dish with a nice cup of coffee or tea for breakfast.

Cinnamon Rolls in the Air Fryer

- This recipe serves 8 people.
- Preparation time: 10 minutes
- Time to cook: 10 minutes.

Nutritional data per serving: 299 calories, 19 grams of carbohydrates, 3 grams of protein, and 18 grams of fat.

Ingredients:

To make the cinnamon rolls:

- 1 tablespoon cinnamon powder
- 100 g (3.5 oz) butter
- 6 teaspoons brown sugar
- 1 sheet frozen puff pastry, thawed

To make the icing:

- 50 g/1.8 oz icing sugar
- Two tablespoons milk

Method:

1. Preheat your air fryer to 200° Celsius (400° Fahrenheit) and line the bottom of the basket with parchment paper.
1. Combine the cinnamon, butter, and brown sugar in a small mixing basin.
2. Roll out the puff pastry sheet and evenly sprinkle with the cinnamon mixture.
3. Cut the puff pastry into 2-inch pieces after rolling it into swirls.
4. Cook the cinnamon roll slices in the air fryer for 7-8 minutes, or until golden and crispy.
5. While the cinnamon rolls are baking, make a thick frosting with the icing sugar and milk. If the mixture seems too dry and crumbly, add a splash of water.
6. When the cinnamon rolls are done, sprinkle the icing sugar evenly over the tops. Leave the set and enjoy it while it's still warm.

English breakfast in the Air Fryer

- This recipe yields 2 servings.
- Preparation time: 5 minutes
- 15 minutes of cooking time.

Nutritional data per serving: 315 calories, 18 grams of carbohydrates, 6 grams of protein, and 12 grams of fat.

Ingredients:

- Two beaten eggs
- two tablespoons milk
- 1 tablespoon melted butter
- 1 teaspoon sea salt
- 1 teaspoon ground black pepper
- Six sausages
- 6 bacon rashers
- 4 little black puddings
- Four big tomatoes
- 1 baked bean can (400 g/14 oz)

Method:

1. Preheat your air fryer to 180° Celsius (350°F) and line the bottom of the basket with parchment paper.
2. Whisk together the eggs, milk, butter, salt, and black pepper in a mixing dish. 3. Fill the air fryer halfway with the mixture.
3. Combine the sausages, bacon rashers, black pudding, and tomatoes in a mixing bowl. 4. Cook for 10 minutes with the cover closed on the air fryer.
4. The egg should be done after 10 minutes. Remove the eggs from the air fryer and replace them with the baked beans.
5. Cook for another 5 minutes.
6. Add more black pepper to the breakfast.

Cheesy Rolls in the Air Fryer

- This recipe serves 8 people.
- 30 minutes for preparation.
- Time to cook: 10 minutes.

Nutritional data per serving: 278 calories, 16 grams of carbohydrates, 8 grams of protein, and 15 grams of fat.

Ingredients:

- 1 tablespoon extra-virgin olive oil
- 8 frankfurters
- 1/2 onions, sliced
- 100 g grated cheddar cheese (3.5 g)
- 100 g grated Parmesan cheese (3.5 g)
- 4 beaten eggs
- 1 tablespoon melted butter
- 1 tablespoon milk
- 1 teaspoon sea salt
- 1/2 teaspoons of black pepper
- 12 wrappers for egg rolls

Method:

- Preheat your air fryer to 180° Celsius (350°F) and line the bottom of the basket with parchment paper.
- In a small pan, heat 1 tablespoon olive oil and fry the sausages and onion slices for 4-5 minutes. Place aside.
- In a mixing dish, combine the cheddar and Parmesan cheeses with the eggs, butter, milk, salt, and black pepper.
- Cut the sausages into tiny pieces and combine them with the onions in the cheese mixture.
- Divide the contents evenly among the egg roll wrappers and tightly roll them up. If required, use cocktail sticks to hold them closed.
- Cook the rolls in the air fryer for 3–4 minutes, or until golden and crispy.
- Serve immediately with salsa or a splash of maple syrup.

Banana Pancakes with Two Ingredients in the Air Fryer

- This recipe yields 2 servings.
- Preparation time: 5 minutes
- Time to cook-10 minutes

Nutritional data per serving: 135 calories, 6 grams of carbohydrates, 4 grams of protein, and 5 grams of fat.

Ingredients:

- Two bananas
- Two beaten eggs

Method:

1. Preheat your air fryer to 180° Celsius (350°F) and line the bottom of the basket with parchment paper.
2. Peel and mash the bananas in a basin with a fork.
3. Stir in the eggs until well mixed.
4. Pour half of the batter into the heated air fryer and spread it out into a pancake on the bottom.
5. Bake for 10 minutes or until the top is golden and crispy.
6. Remove the pancake with care and set it aside. Steps 4 and 5 should be repeated with the leftover batter.
7. Serve the pancakes hot with maple syrup, additional banana slices, strawberry slices, or any other desired toppings.

French toast in the Air Fryer

- This recipe yields 2 servings.
- Preparation time: 10 minutes
- 5 minutes of cooking time.

Per serving, there are 256 calories, 16 grams of carbohydrates, 5 grams of protein, and 5 grams of fat.

Ingredients:

- 4 bread slices.
- Four eggs
- Milk (200 mL)
- 2 teaspoons of sugar
- 1 tbsp. vanilla extract
- 1/2 teaspoon cinnamon powder
- 1 teaspoon maple syrup

Method:

1. Preheat your air fryer to 150° Celsius (300° Fahrenheit) and line the bottom of the basket with parchment paper.
2. Cut the bread into two rectangles. Place aside.
3. Whisk together the 4 eggs, milk, sugar, vanilla extract, and powdered cinnamon in a mixing dish.
4. Soak the bread slices in the egg mixture until completely coated. They should just take around 2 minutes.
1. Place the moistened bread slices in the air fryer baskets, cover, and cook for 4-5 minutes.
5. Drizzle the French toast with maple syrup and top with additional sugar if desired.

Pop Tarts with Fruit from the Air Fryer

- This recipe serves 8 people.
- Preparation time: 15 minutes
- Time to cook: 10 minutes.

Nutritional data per serving: 234 calories, 28 grams of carbohydrates, 3 grams of protein, and 12 grams of fat.

Ingredients

To make the filling:

- 100 g (3.5 oz) fresh blueberries
- 50 g of fresh raspberries (1.8 oz).
- Fresh strawberries, 50 g (1.8 oz.)
- 100 g sugar (3.5 oz)
- 1 tbsp corn starch
- To make the pastry:
- 1 sheet puff pastry

For the icing:

- Four tbsp powdered sugar
- 2 tablespoons of berry compote or maple syrup
- 1 teaspoon of lemon juice

Method:

1. Preheat your air fryer to 180° Celsius (350°F) and line the bottom of the basket with parchment paper.
6. Begin by combining the blueberries, strawberries, raspberries, and sugar in a large saucepan set over medium heat. Bring the mixture to a boil, stirring constantly and breaking up the berries.
2. Stir in the corn starch and cook for another 1-2 minutes. Take the pan off the heat and put it aside.
3. Roll out the puff pastry sheet and cut it into 8 equal rectangles to form the pastry.
4. Spread 2 tbsp of berry filling on one side of each rectangle. To cover the filling, fold the opposite side of each puff pastry rectangle over. Seal the edges with a fork.
7. Place the filled puff pastry rectangles in the air fryer basket. Cook for 10 minutes, or until the crust is golden and crispy. After removing from the air fryer, set aside to cool.
8. Make the frosting while the puff pastry rectangles are cooling by combining the powdered sugar, maple syrup, and lemon juice in a mixing dish. Whisk vigorously until the mixture is smooth.
9. Drizzle the icing over the cooled pop tarts and serve!

LUNCH RECIPES

Turkey Burgers in the Air Fryer

- This recipe serves 4 people.
- Preparation time: 5 minutes
- 15 minutes of cooking time.

Per serving, there are 310 calories, 14 grams of carbohydrates, 21 grams of protein, and 10 grams of fat.

Ingredients:

- 400 g/14 oz. ground turkey
- 1 tbsp. Cajun seasoning
- 1 tablespoon cumin
- 1 tsp. onion powder
- 1 tablespoon garlic powder
- 2 teaspoons dried mixed herbs
- 1/2 teaspoon of salt.
- 1/2 teaspoons of black pepper
- 1 egg, beaten
- 1 teaspoon of soy sauce

Method:

1. Preheat your air fryer to 200° Celsius (400° Fahrenheit) and line the bottom of the basket with parchment paper.
2. Combine the ground turkey, Cajun spice, onion powder, garlic powder, dried mixed herbs, salt, and black pepper in a mixing bowl. Mix until well combined.
3. Stir in the eggs and soy sauce until all of the ingredients are completely combined.
4. Form the mixture into four equal patties. Cook for 15-20 minutes, flipping halfway through, until the patties are thoroughly cooked in the preheated air fryer basket. Burgers should be golden brown and crunchy.
5. Serve the patties on burger buns with additional salad and your favorite's sauce.

Lemon Cod in the Air Fryer

- This recipe serves 4 people.
- Preparation time: 5 minutes
- Time to cook: 10 minutes.

Per serving, there are 185 calories, 4 grams of carbohydrates, 19 grams of protein, and 6 grams of fat.

Ingredients:

- 4 fillets of cod (100 g/3.5 ounce)
- 3 tablespoons of melted unsalted butter.
- 1 lemon, peeled and cut in half
- 1/ teaspoon of salt
- 1/2 teaspoons of black pepper

Method:

1. Preheat your air fryer to 200° Celsius (400° Fahrenheit) and line the bottom of the basket with parchment paper.
1. Place the fillets of fish on a clean surface. Use a pastry brush to coat the tops of the fillets with melted butter.
2. Squeeze the juice of half a lemon over the top of each buttered fish fillet, and season with salt and black pepper to taste.
3. Cut the remaining half of the lemon into slices and place one on each fish fillet.
4. Place the fillets in the air fryer, cover, and cook for 10 minutes, or until the fish is soft and flaky.
5. Serve the fish right away with fresh potatoes and vegetables.

Chicken Wings in the Air

- This recipe serves 4 people.
- Preparation time: 10 minutes
- Time to cook: 20 minutes.

Nutritional data per serving: 99 calories, 6 grams of carbohydrates, 2 grams of protein, and 6 grams of fat.

Ingredients:

- Chicken wings (400 g/14 oz)
- 1 teaspoon sea salt
- 1 teaspoon ground black pepper
- 4 tablespoons of spicy sauce
- 4 tablespoons of olive oil.
- 1 teaspoon of soy sauce
- 1 tablespoon garlic powder

Method:

1. Preheat your air fryer to 200° Celsius (400° Fahrenheit) and line the bottom of the basket with parchment paper.
2. Season the wings with salt and pepper. Put them in the air fryer, shut the top, and cook for 12–15 minutes.
3. In the meanwhile, combine the spicy sauce, olive oil, soy sauce, and garlic powder in a mixing bowl. To make a sauce, combine all of the ingredients in a mixing bowl.
4. Remove the chicken wings from the air fryer and throw them in the spicy sauce mixture, coating each wing well.
1. Return the wings to the air fryer and cook for 5 minutes more.
5. Serve the wings while they are still hot.

Tofu Sticky from the Air Fryer

- This recipe serves 4 people.
- 30 minutes for preparation.
- 15 minutes of cooking time.

Nutritional data per serving: 299 calories, 8 grammes of carbohydrates, 13 grammes of protein, and 5 grammes of fat.

Ingredients:

- 1 tsp. onion powder
- 1 tablespoon garlic powder
- 1 tbsp. smoked paprika
- 2 tbsp of soy sauce
- 2 tbsp. sweet chili sauce
- 2 tbsp Sriracha sauce
- 400 g/14 oz diced firm block tofu
- Three tbsp corn starch
- 1 teaspoon ground black pepper

Method:

1. Preheat your air fryer to 150° Celsius (300° Fahrenheit) and line the bottom of the basket with parchment paper.
2. In a small mixing bowl, combine the onion powder, garlic powder, smoked paprika, soy sauce, sweet chili sauce, and sriracha. Combine thoroughly.
3. Toss the tofu pieces in the sauce to coat them evenly. Marinate for 20 minutes in the refrigerator.
6. Combine the corn starch and pepper in a mixing dish. Coat the tofu in the corn starch mixture and place it in the air fryer basket that has been prepared.
4. Close the machine's top and cook the tofu cubes for 15 minutes, or until golden and crispy.
5. Serve immediately with sweeter chili sauce and a side of noodles and vegetables.

Crab Cakes in the Air Fryer with Tartar Sauce

- This recipe serves 4 people.
- Preparation time: 20 minutes
- 15 minutes of cooking time.

Nutritional data per serving: 243 calories, 11 grams of carbohydrates, 13 grams of protein, and 8 grams of fat.

Ingredients:

- To make the crab cakes:
- 3 teaspoons mayonnaise
- ONE EGG
- 2 teaspoons dried mixed herbs
- 2 teaspoons Dijon mustard
- 1 tsp. lemon zest
- 1 teaspoon salt
- Crab meat, 400 g (14 oz.)
- 8 smashed whole meal crackers.

To make the tartar sauce:

- 4 teaspoons mayonnaise
- 1/2 shallots, finely chopped
- 2 tablespoons coarsely chopped capers
- 1 tsp. lemon juice
- 1/2 teaspoons of Dijon mustard
- 1 teaspoon fresh dill, coarsely chopped

Method:

1. To make the crab cakes, combine the mayonnaise, egg, dried mixed herbs, Dijon mustard, lemon zest, and salt in a mixing bowl.
2. Gently fold in the crab meat and whole meal crackers until evenly coated in sauce.
3. Shape the mixture into 8 evenly sized patties and chill for 15 minutes.
4. Preheat your air fryer to 200° Celsius (400° Fahrenheit) and line the bottom of the basket with parchment paper.
5. Remove the crab cakes from the refrigerator and set them in the air fryer basket that has been lined. Cook the patties for 15 minutes, turning halfway.
6. In the meanwhile, create the tartar sauce by whisking together all of the ingredients in a small mixing dish.
7. Serve the crab cakes warm, with tartar sauce and your choice of side.

Falafel in the Air Fryer with Tahini Sauce

- This recipe serves 4 people.
- Preparation time: 10 minutes
- 15 minutes of cooking time.

Nutritional data per serving: 178 calories, 12 grams of carbohydrates, 10 grams of protein, and 9 grams of fat.

Ingredients:

To make the falafel:

- 1/2 onions, sliced
- 4 garlic cloves peeled and sliced.
- 2 tbsp fresh parsley, chopped
- 2 tbsp fresh coriander, chopped
- 2 400 g/14 oz washed and drained chickpeas
- 1 teaspoon sea salt
- 1 tsp. baking powder
- 1 tbsp. dried mixed herbs
- 1/2 tablespoons red pepper flakes, crushed

To make the tahini sauce:

- 3 tablespoons of tahini.
- 1/2 oz. lemon juice
- 3 tablespoons of water, plus more if necessary,

Method:

1. Preheat your air fryer to 180° Celsius (350°F) and line the bottom of the basket with parchment paper.
2. In a food processor, combine the onion, garlic cloves, fresh parsley, and fresh coriander. Pulse the mixture for 30 seconds at a time until it is well mixed, scraping the sides of the food processor as needed.
3. Combine the chickpeas, salt, baking powder, dried mixed herbs, and crushed red pepper flakes in a mixing bowl.
4. Pulse the mixture until it is well blended. If required, add extra water. The mixture should be crumbly but not dry. It should have a paste-like texture.
5. Scoop out 2 tablespoons of the ingredients at a time and form into little balls. Cook for 15 minutes with the falafel balls in the preheated air fryer basket.
6. Make the tahini sauce while the falafels are cooking by putting all of the ingredients in a dish.
7. Drizzle tahini sauce over the falafels and serve hot or cold. Serve with whole meal pita bread and salad to make the wheat more substantial.

Salmon Patties in the Air Fryer

- This recipe serves 4 people.
- Preparation time: 15 minutes
- Time to cook: 10 minutes.

Nutritional data per serving: 276 calories, 10 grams of carbohydrates, 18 grams of protein, and 15 grams of fat.

Ingredients:

- 1 x 400 g/14 oz canned salmon, drained and crushed
- Two eggs
- 4 teaspoons mayonnaise
- 1 teaspoon sea salt
- 100 g (3.5 oz) breadcrumbs
- 2 tbsp unsweetened yoghurt
- 1 lemon, freshly squeezed

Method:

1. Preheat your air fryer to 180° Celsius (350°F) and line the bottom of the basket with parchment paper.
2. Combine the salmon, eggs, mayonnaise, salt, breadcrumbs, yoghurt, and lemon juice in a large mixing dish.
3. Using your hands, form small portions of the ingredients into patties. Make sure the patties are no more than 1 inch thick and that they are all the same thickness.
4. Cook the patties for 10 minutes in the air fryer, flipping halfway through. The patties should be brown and crispy on the outside.
5. Serve with a side salad and extra yoghurt to dip your burgers in.

Pockets of Air Fryer Ham and Egg Pastry

- This recipe yields 2 servings.
- Preparation time: 15 minutes
- 15 minutes of cooking time.

Nutritional data per serving: 335 calories, 23 grammes of carbohydrates, 10 grammes of protein, and 18 grammes of fat.

Ingredients:

- ONE EGG
- two tablespoons milk
- 2 tablespoons of butter.
- Diced ham (400 g/14 oz)
- 50 g grated cheddar cheese (3.5 oz)
- 2 rolled crescents.

Method:

1. Preheat your air fryer to 180° Celsius (350°F) and line the bottom of the basket with parchment paper.
2. In a small dish, whisk together 1 egg and 2 tablespoons of milk.
3. In a pan, melt 2 tablespoons of butter and add the egg mixture. Cook the eggs for 5 minutes, or until they are set and scrambled.
4. Take the eggs from the stove and set them in a basin. Mix in the ham and cheddar cheese.
5. Divide half of the filling among the crescent rolls. To cover the filling, fold the rolls over and squeeze the corners to close.
6. Close the cover and bake for 8 to 10 minutes, or until the crescent rolls are golden brown and slightly crispy on the sides.

FAVORITES FOR LUNCH

Chicken Parmesan in the Air Fryer

- This recipe serves 4 people.
- Preparation time: 15 minutes
- Time to cook: 10 minutes.

Nutritional data per serving: 297 calories, 13 grams of carbohydrates, 14 grams of protein, and 11 grams of fat.

Ingredients:

- Skinless, boneless chicken breasts (400 g/14 oz)
- 1 teaspoon sea salt
- 1 teaspoon ground black pepper
- Parmesan cheese, 50 g/1.8 oz
- 100 g/3.5 oz unbleached flour
- Two eggs
- 100 g / 3.5 oz Panko breadcrumbs
- 1/2 teaspoons of garlic powder
- 1/2 teaspoons of onion powder
- 1/2 teaspoons of dried oregano
- 8 tablespoons of marinara sauce
- 100 g (3.5 oz) grated cheddar

Method:

1. Preheat your air fryer to 200° Celsius (400° Fahrenheit) and line the bottom of the basket with parchment paper.
2. Salt and pepper the chicken breasts and cut them in half.
3. In a small bowl, combine the Parmesan cheese, garlic powder, onion powder, and dried oregano. Stuff each chicken breast with the Parmesan cheese mixture and press the sides down to seal the mixture within the breasts.
1. Place the flour in a small mixing dish, whisk the eggs in a second bowl, and combine the panko breadcrumbs in a third.
4. Coat the chicken breasts in flour, then in the egg mixture, then in the panko breadcrumbs. By the end, the breadcrumbs should have completely covered the chicken breasts.
5. Cook the chicken breasts in the air fryer basket for 5 minutes. Cook for a further 5 minutes, or until the chicken is crispy and golden and the cheese has melted on top of each chicken breast.
6. Meanwhile, cook the marinara sauce in a heat-resistant bowl for 30-60 seconds, or until hot.
7. Drizzle the chicken with the hot marinara sauce.

Air Fryer Cod with Lemon and Dill

- This recipe serves 4 people.
- Preparation time: 10 minutes
- Time to cook-10 minutes

Nutritional information per serving: 302 calories, 5 grams of carbohydrates, 30 grams of protein, and 12 grams of fat.

Ingredients:

- 4 fillets of cod (100 g/3.5 ounce)
- 4 tablespoons melted butter
- 6 peeled and chopped garlic cloves.
- 2 teaspoons lemon juice
- 2 tbsp fresh dill, coarsely chopped
- 1/2 teaspoon of salt

Method:

1. Preheat your air fryer to 180° Celsius (350°F) and line the bottom of the basket with parchment paper.
2. Arrange the fillets of fish on a clean surface.
3. Combine the butter, garlic cloves, lemon juice, fresh dill, and salt in a mixing dish.
4. Put a spoonful of the garlic butter mixture on top of each fillet of cod and gently press down to keep the filling from falling off while the fish is cooking.
5. Place the fish fillets in the air fryer basket that has been lined. Check that they don't overlap one another.
6. Close the cover of the air fryer and cook for 10 minutes, or until the fish is done. When you break it with a fork, it should fall apart.
7. Serve the cod fillets right away with rice and vegetables.

Garlic Butter Air Fryer Steak

- This recipe yields 2 servings.
- Preparation time: 10 minutes
- 15 minutes of cooking time.

Nutritional data per serving: 414 calories, 9 grams of carbohydrates, 15 grams of protein, and 10 grams of fat.

Ingredients:

- 4 tablespoons softened butter
- 2 peeled and chopped garlic cloves.
- 2 tsp fresh chopped parsley
- 1 teaspoon fresh chives, chopped
- 1 teaspoon fresh thyme, chopped
- 1 tbsp. dried oregano
- Rib-eye steak (800 g/28 oz)
- 1 teaspoon sea salt
- 1 teaspoon ground black pepper

Method:

1. Preheat your air fryer to 200° Celsius (400° Fahrenheit) and line the bottom of the basket with parchment paper.
2. In a mixing dish, combine the butter, chopped garlic, parsley, chives, thyme, and oregano.
3. Using an egg brush, gently cover both sides of the steak with the garlic butter mixture. The majority of the mixture will be used for the garlic butter, so don't use it all.
4. Freeze the leftover garlic butter to solidify while the steaks cook.
5. Put the steak in the air fryer basket, close the lid, and cook for 15 minutes, flipping halfway.
6. Take the steaks out of the air fryer and spoon some of the slightly solidified garlic butter into the Centre of each one.
7. Arrange chips and salad on the side.

Roast Pork on the Air Fryer

- This recipe serves 4 people.
- Preparation time: 20 minutes
- 15 minutes of cooking time.

456 calories per serving, 12 grams of carbohydrates, 18 grams of protein, and 9 grams of fat.

Ingredients:

- One big hunk of pork
- 1 teaspoon sea salt
- 1 teaspoon ground black pepper

Method:

1. Using a sharp knife, score the pork loin.
2. Dry the rind with a paper towel and massage in the salt and black pepper.
3. Chill the pork loin for 20 minutes.
4. Preheat your air fryer to 200° Celsius (400° Fahrenheit) and line the bottom of the basket with parchment paper.
5. Cook the pork loin in the air fryer for 15 minutes, skin side up, or until brown and crispy.
6. Set aside for 15 minutes to cool before cutting into pieces.

Naan Pizzas in the Air Fryer

- This recipe yields 2 servings.
- Preparation time: 5 minutes
- 5 minutes of cooking time.

Nutritional data per serving: 298 calories, 15 grams of carbohydrates, 9 grams of protein, and 8 grams of fat.

Ingredients:

- Two naan flatbreads, plain
- 2 tablespoons spaghetti tomato
- 50 g grated cheddar cheese (1.8 oz)
- 1 tbsp. dried mixed herbs

Method:

1. Preheat your air fryer to 190° Celsius (375° Fahrenheit) and line the bottom of the basket with parchment paper.
1. Spread 1 tbsp tomato paste on each naan.
2. Top with cheddar cheese and dried mixed herbs.
3. Place the naan bread pizzas in the prepared air fryer basket, cover, and cook for 5 minutes, or until the naans are golden and crispy and the cheese has melted.

Sausage Biscuits in the Air Fryer

- This recipe serves 4 people.
- Preparation time: 5 minutes
- Time to cook: 20 minutes.

Nutritional data per serving: 189 calories, 5 grams of carbohydrates, 7 grams of protein, and 10 grams of fat.

Ingredients:

- 1 tablespoon extra-virgin olive oil
- 14 oz (400 g) of sausage meat.
- Two eggs
- 1/2 teaspoon of salt
- 1/2 teaspoons of black pepper
- 100 g (3.5 oz) grated cheddar
- (14 oz) 400 g flaky biscuits

Method:

1. In a pan, heat the olive oil and add the sausages. Cook for 8-10 minutes, or until golden. Set it on paper towels to drain.
2. Whisk together the eggs, salt, and black pepper in a mixing dish. 3. Cook for 4-5 minutes, until the eggs are gently cooked and scrambled in a heated skillet. They will not be entirely cooked at this stage, but will continue to cook when put in the air fryer.
3. Preheat your air fryer to 180° Celsius (350°F) and line the bottom of the basket with parchment paper.
4. Arrange half of the flaky biscuits on a plate and top with shredded cheddar cheese evenly. Spread the sausage meat and egg mixture equally on top.
5. Place the remaining half of the flaky biscuits on top and squeeze the edges together to seal the filled side.
6. Place the stuffed biscuits in the air fryer basket and cook for 5 minutes, or until golden brown.
7. Eat the sausage biscuits while they're still hot.

Lemon shrimp in the air fryer

- This recipe serves 4 people.
- Preparation time: 5 minutes
- Time to cook: 10 minutes.

Nutritional information per serving: 334 calories, 3 grams of carbohydrates, 16 grams of protein, and 12 grams of fat.

Ingredients:

- Uncooked shrimp, 400 g/14 ounces, peeled and deveined.
- 2 tablespoons of olive oil.
- 2 teaspoons lemon juice
- 1 teaspoon sea salt
- 1 teaspoon ground black pepper

Method:

1. Preheat your air fryer to 200° Celsius (400° Fahrenheit) and line the bottom of the basket with parchment paper.
2. Combine the shrimp, olive oil, lemon juice, salt, and black pepper in a mixing dish.
3. Toss to coat the shrimp completely.
4. Place the shrimp in the air fryer basket and cook for 7-8 minutes, or until the shells become pink and the shrimp is somewhat opaque.
5. Take the shrimp out of the air fryer and serve them with your preferred sides.

Fried Chicken on the Air Fryer

- This recipe serves 8 people.
- Preparation time: 10 minutes
- Time to cook: 20 minutes.

445 calories per serving, 23 grams of carbohydrates, 25 grams of protein, and 18 grams of fat.

Ingredients:

- Buttermilk (200 mL)
- Two eggs
- Bone-in chicken thighs, 800 g/28 oz.
- Plain flour (200 g/7 oz)
- 2 paprika teaspoons
- 1 tablespoon chili powder, mild
- 2 tablespoons garlic powder
- 2 tablespoons onion powder
- 1 teaspoon sea salt
- 1 teaspoon ground black pepper

Method:

1. Preheat your air fryer to 200° Celsius (400° Fahrenheit) and line the bottom of the basket with parchment paper.
1. In a large mixing basin, whisk together the buttermilk and eggs until thoroughly blended.
2. Combine the plain flour, paprika, chili powder, garlic powder, onion powder, salt, and black pepper in a separate bowl. Combine thoroughly.
3. Dip the chicken into the wet mixture, then the dry mixture, to completely cover each thigh with spices.
4. Place the chicken thighs in the air fryer basket that has been prepared. Cook for 20 minutes, or until the chicken thighs are crispy.
5. Serve immediately with your favorites side dishes.

Air Fryer Chicken in the South

- This recipe serves 4 people.
- Preparation time: 15 minutes
- 15 minutes of cooking time.

Nutritional data per serving: 372 calories, 17 grams of carbohydrates, 21 grams of protein, and 13 grams of fat.

Ingredients:

- Crackers, 200 g/7 oz.
- 1 teaspoon fresh parsley, chopped
- 1 paprika teaspoon
- 1 tsp. chili powder
- 1 teaspoon sea salt
- ONE EGG
- Chicken thighs (400 g/14 oz)

Method:

1. Preheat your air fryer to 180° Celsius (350°F) and line the bottom of the basket with parchment paper.
2. In a mixing bowl, crush the cracks until they resemble breadcrumbs.
3. Combine the fresh parsley, paprika, chilli powder, and salt in a mixing bowl.
4. Mix everything up well.
5. Crack the egg into a separate basin and whisk thoroughly.
6. Dip the chicken thighs into the egg, then into the cracker-spice mixture. Ensure that the thighs are completely coated with breadcrumbs on both sides.
7. Cook the chicken thighs for 12–15 minutes in the air fryer basket, or until golden and crispy.

Air Fryer Meatballs with a Sweet and Sticky Sauce

- This recipe serves 4 people.
- 30 minutes for preparation.
- 15 minutes of cooking time.

Nutritional data per serving: 257 calories, 16 grammes of carbohydrates, 19 grammes of protein, and 11 grammes of fat.

Ingredients:

To make the meatballs:

- 200 g of rolled oats (7 oz)
- 100 g / 3.5 oz crackers
- Two beaten eggs
- 1 gallon evaporated milk
- 1 teaspoon onion powder
- 1 teaspoon garlic powder
- 1 teaspoon sea salt
- 1 tablespoon ground cumin
- 800 g ground minced beef (28 oz)

To make the sauce:

- 4 tablespoons of brown sugar.
- three tablespoons honey
- 2 teaspoons corn starch
- 3 tbsp of soy sauce
- 2 tbsp. Worcestershire sauce

Method:

1. Preheat your air fryer to 180° Celsius (350°F) and line the bottom of the basket with parchment paper.
2. Rolling oats, crackers, eggs, evaporated milk, onion powder, garlic powder, salt, ground cumin, Stir until completely blended.
3. Fold in the meat gently.
4. Form the ingredients into tiny, uniform meatballs. Place in the air fryer basket that has been preheated. Cook the meatballs for 12–15 minutes, or until golden and browned.
5. Make the sauce while the meatballs are cooking by thoroughly mixing all of the ingredients in a saucepan. Heat the ingredients until the sauce thickens and becomes hot all the way through.
6. Serve the meatballs hot with the sweet and sticky sauce on top. Make it a substantial lunchtime entrée by adding rice and veggies.

SIDES DESHES

Garlic Bread in the Air Fryer

- This recipe serves 8 people.
- Preparation time: 5 minutes
- 5 minutes of cooking time.

Per serving, there are 137 calories, 15 grammes of carbohydrates, 4 grammes of protein, and 9 grammes of fat.

Ingredients:

- 4 tablespoons softened butter
- 2 peeled and chopped garlic cloves.
- 2 teaspoons fresh chopped parsley
- 8 ciabatta bread pieces.
- 3 tbsp Parmesan cheese, grated

Method:

1. Preheat your air fryer to 180° Celsius (350°F) and line the bottom of the basket with parchment paper.
2. In a mixing dish, combine the butter, garlic cloves, and fresh parsley.
3. Evenly distribute the garlic-butter mixture over the 8 ciabatta pieces. Grate Parmesan cheese on top.
1. Place the ciabatta pieces in the air fryer, cover, and cook for 5 minutes or until golden and crispy and the cheese has melted.

Chickpeas Crispy from the Air Fryer

- This recipe serves 4 people.
- Preparation time: 5 minutes
- 15 minutes of cooking time.

Nutritional data per serving: 131 calories, 15 grammes of carbohydrates, 8 grammes of protein, and 4 grammes of fat.

Ingredients:

- 1 cans chickpeas (400 g/14 oz)
- 1 tablespoon extra-virgin olive oil
- 1 tbsp. smoked paprika
- 1 tbsp. Cajun seasoning
- 1 tbsp. cayenne pepper
- 1 teaspoon ground black pepper

Method:

1. Preheat your air fryer to 200° Celsius (400° Fahrenheit) and line the bottom of the basket with parchment paper.
2. Drain and rinse the chickpeas with cool water.
3. Put them together in a large mixing dish.
4. Combine the olive oil, smoked paprika, Cajun spice, cayenne pepper, and black pepper in a mixing bowl. 4. Toss the chickpeas in the oil and spices to coat well.
5. Air-fry the chickpeas for 12–15 minutes, or until golden and crispy.
6. Serve with your favorites vegetables for lunch.

Potatoes in the Air Fryer

- This recipe serves 4 people.
- Preparation time: 5 minutes
- 15 minutes of cooking time.

Nutritional data per serving: 120 calories, 19 grammes of carbohydrates, 4 grammes of protein, and 5 grammes of fat.

Ingredients:

- 400 g/14 oz baby fresh potatoes, halved
- 1 tablespoon extra-virgin olive oil
- 1 tablespoon garlic powder
- 1 tbsp. dried mixed herbs
- 1 teaspoon Cajun spice
- 1/2 teaspoon of salt
- 1/2 teaspoons of black pepper

Method:

1. Preheat your air fryer to 200° Celsius (400° Fahrenheit) and line the bottom of the basket with parchment paper.
2. Toss the potatoes with the olive oil, garlic powder, dried mixed herbs, Cajun powder, salt, and pepper in a large mixing basin.
3. Place the potatoes in your air fryer's prepared basket, cover the lid, and cook for 15 minutes.
4. Serve immediately as a side dish with your main course.

Sweet Potato Fries in the Air Fryer

- This recipe serves 4 people.
- Preparation time: 5 minutes
- Time to cook - 10 minutes

Nutritional data per serving: 111 calories, 18 grammes of carbohydrates, 3 grammes of protein, and 4 grammes of fat.

Ingredients:

- 2 peeled sweet potatoes.
- 2 tablespoons of olive oil.
- 1 teaspoon sea salt
- 1 teaspoon ground black pepper
- 1 paprika teaspoon
- 1 tablespoon garlic powder

Method:

1. Preheat your air fryer to 200° Celsius (400° Fahrenheit) and line the bottom of the basket with parchment paper.
1. Place the sweet potatoes in a large mixing dish and cut them into wedges.
2. In a mixing bowl, combine the olive oil, salt, black pepper, paprika, and garlic powder. Toss the potato wedges in the oil and spices to coat.
3. Cook the sweet potato wedges in the air fryer for 10 minutes, flipping halfway through, until crispy.

Mixed Vegetables in the Air Fryer

- This recipe serves 4 people.
- Preparation time: 10 minutes
- Time to cook: 20 minutes.

Nutritional data per serving: 99 calories, 15 grammes of carbohydrates, 3 grammes of protein, and 5 grammes of fat.

Ingredients:

- 100 g (3.5 oz) halved Brussels sprouts
- 1 aubergine, sliced
- 1 red pepper, sliced
- 2 big peeled and sliced carrots.
- 2 tablespoons of olive oil.
- 1 tbsp. balsamic vinegar
- 2 teaspoons dried mixed herbs
- 1/2 teaspoon of salt
- 1/2 teaspoons of black pepper

Method:

- Preheat your air fryer to 200° Celsius (400° Fahrenheit) and line the bottom of the basket with parchment paper.
- Toss the chopped veggies with the olive oil, balsamic vinegar, dried mixed herbs, salt, and black pepper in a large mixing dish. 3.
- Cook the vegetables in the air fryer for 15-20 minutes or until soft and tender.
- Serve with your main course.

Broccoli in the Air Fryer

- This recipe yields 2 servings.
- Preparation time: 10 minutes
- Time to cook: 10 minutes.

Per serving, there are 65 calories, 5 grammes of carbohydrates, 2 grammes of protein, and 4 grammes of fat.

Ingredients:

- 1 broccoli floret, broken.
- 1 tablespoon extra-virgin olive oil
- 1 peeled and minced garlic clove
- 1 teaspoon sea salt
- 1 teaspoon ground black pepper

Method:

1. Preheat your air fryer to 180° Celsius (350°F) and line the bottom of the basket with parchment paper.
2. In a mixing bowl, combine the broccoli florets, olive oil, garlic, salt, and black pepper. Toss to coat the broccoli completely.
3. Cook the broccoli in the air fryer for 10 minutes, or until tender.

Air Fryer Buffalo Cauliflower with Blue Cheese Sauce

- This recipe yields 2 servings.
- Preparation time: 10 minutes
- 15 minutes of cooking time.

Nutritional data per serving: 167 calories, 10 grammes of carbohydrates, 4 grammes of protein, and 9 grammes of fat.

Ingredients:

To prepare the cauliflower:

- 1 cauliflower, peeled and cut into florets
- 3 tablespoons hot sauce
- 3 tablespoons melted butter
- 1/2 teaspoons of garlic powder
- 1/2 teaspoon of salt
- 1/2 teaspoons of black pepper
- 1teaspoon cornstarch

For the blue cheese sauce, combine the following ingredients:

- Crumbled blue cheese 50 g/1.8 oz
- 2 tbsp. soured cream
- 3 teaspoons mayonnaise
- 1/2 teaspoon of salt
- 1/2 teaspoons of black pepper

Method:

- Preheat your air fryer to 180° Celsius (350°F) and line the bottom of the basket with parchment paper.
- Combine the spicy sauce, melted butter, garlic powder, salt, and black pepper in a large mixing bowl.
- Toss the cauliflower in the basin to coat it.
- Sprinkle the corn starch over the cauliflower and toss to combine.
- Place the cauliflower in the air fryer machine's prepared basket, shut the lid, and cook for 15 minutes, or until golden and crispy.
- Make the blue-cheese sauce while the cauliflower is cooking. In a small mixing dish, combine all of the ingredients.
- Remove the cauliflower from the air fryer and serve with a side of blue cheese sauce.

Honey Carrots in the Air Fryer

- This recipe serves 4 people.
- Preparation time: 10 minutes
- 15 minutes of cooking time.

Nutritional data per serving: 120 calories, 13 grammes of carbohydrates, 4 grammes of protein, and 5 grammes of fat.

Ingredients:

- 4 big peeled and sliced carrots.
- 1 tablespoon extra-virgin olive oil
- Two tablespoons honey
- 1 teaspoon ground black pepper

Method:

1. Preheat your air fryer to 150° Celsius (300° Fahrenheit) and line the bottom of the basket with parchment paper.
2. Toss the carrots in a bowl with the olive oil, honey, and black pepper. Toss to coat the carrots completely.
3. Put the carrots in the air fryer basket that has been prepared, close the lid, and cook for 20 minutes, or until the carrots are soft in the middle but crispy on the edges.

Fried rice in the air fryer

- This recipe serves 4 people.
- Preparation time: 5 minutes
- 15 minutes of cooking time.

Nutritional data per serving: 201 calories, 15 grammes of carbohydrates, 10 grammes of protein, and 6 grammes of fat.

Ingredients:

- 400 g of cooked brown rice (14 oz).
- 100 g/3.5 oz frozen mixed vegetables
- 1 tablespoon extra-virgin olive oil
- 2 scrambled eggs.

Method:

1. Preheat your air fryer to 150° Celsius (300° Fahrenheit) and line the bottom of the basket with parchment paper.
2. In a mixing dish, combine the cooked rice and frozen veggies.
3. Toss the rice with the olive oil to coat it. Stir in the scrambled eggs.
4. Place the rice mixture in the air fryer and cook for 15 minutes.

DESSERT AND SNACKS RECIPES

Oatmeal and Chocolate Chip Cookies in the Air Fryer

- This recipe serves 8 people.
- Preparation time: 10 minutes
- 15 minutes of cooking time.

Nutritional data per serving: 112 calories, 14 grammes of carbohydrates, 5 grammes of protein, and 10 grammes of fat.

Ingredients:

- 4 tablespoons softened butter
- 100 g sugar (3.5 oz)
- 100 g (3.5 oz) brown sugar
- Two beaten eggs
- 1 tbsp. vanilla extract
- 400 g of rolled oats (14 oz).
- 4 tbsp plain unsweetened yoghurt
- 1 teaspoon sea salt
- 200 g (7 oz) milk chocolate chips
- 2 tbsp. chopped mixed nuts

Method:

1. Preheat your air fryer to 180° Celsius (350°F) and line the bottom of the basket with parchment paper.
2. In a large mixing bowl, cream together the butter and both sugars until light and fluffy.
3. Whisk in the eggs and vanilla extract until smooth.
4. Stir in the rolled oats, yoghurt, and salt, chocolate chips, and chopped mixed nuts.
5. Roll the dough into tiny balls and flatten them into cookies.
6. Close the cover and place the cookies in the prepared air fryer basket.
7. Bake for 8 to 10 minutes or until the cookies are firm, golden, and crunchy around the edges.
8. Remove from the oven and let cool. Serve the cookies cold or warm by reheating them in the microwave.

Banana Bread in the Air Fryer

- This recipe serves 4 people.
- Preparation time: 10 minutes
- 1 hour and 10 minutes of cooking time.

Nutritional data per serving: 154 calories, 15 grammes of carbohydrates, 5 grammes of protein, and 9 grammes of fat.

Ingredients:

- 100 g/3.5 oz unbleached flour
- 1 teaspoon ground cinnamon
- 1 teaspoon nutmeg, ground
- 1/2 teaspoons of baking powder
- 1/2 teaspoon of salt
- 2 peeled ripe bananas.
- Two beaten eggs
- 100 g sugar (3.5 oz)
- four tablespoons milk
- 2 tablespoons of olive oil.
- 1 tbsp. vanilla extract
- 50 g (3.5 oz) of chopped walnuts

Method:

1. Preheat your air fryer to 150° Celsius (300° Fahrenheit) and line a loaf pan with parchment paper.
2. Combine the plain flour, ground cinnamon, powdered nutmeg, baking powder, and salt in a large mixing basin.
3. In a separate dish, mash the ripe bananas well. Crack the eggs into the bowl and thoroughly mix them in. Combine the sugar, milk, olive oil, and vanilla essence in a mixing bowl.
4. Fold the dry components into the wet ones and blend well.
5. Pour the batter into the loaf pan and sprinkle with walnuts. Cook for 30–40 minutes, or until the tin has set, in the air fryer basket. Insert a knife into the cake's Centre. When the cake is entirely baked, it should come out dry.
6. Remove the loaf pan from the air fryer and set it aside to cool before slicing and serving.

Nutella Wedges in the Air Fryer

- This recipe serves 4 people.
- Preparation time: 15 minutes
- Time to cook: 10 minutes.

Nutritional data per serving: 99 calories, 12 grammes of carbohydrates, 3 grammes of protein, and 10 grammes of fat.

Ingredients:

- ONE EGG
- 1 teaspoon of water
- (14 oz) 400 g flaky biscuits
- 4 tablespoons Nutella

Method:

1. Preheat your air fryer to 150° Celsius (300° Fahrenheit) and line the bottom of the basket with parchment paper.
2. In a separate dish, whisk together the egg and 1 tablespoon of water.
3. Roll out the biscuits on a clean, lightly floured board. Divide the dough into four big wedges.
4. Brush each wedge lightly with the egg mixture.
5. Spread 1 tablespoon of Nutella in the Centre of each biscuit wedge.
6. Carefully fold the wedges over, being careful not to fracture the dough. Pinch the corners of the dough together to form little Nutella-filled pockets.
7. Cook the wedges for 8–10 minutes in the air fryer, flipping halfway through.
8. Serve the wedges while they are still hot.

Chocolate Peanut Butter Cake in the Air Fryer

- This recipe serves 4 people.
- Preparation time: 10 minutes
- 15 minutes of cooking time.

Nutritional data per serving: 314 calories, 12 grammes of carbohydrates, 6 grammes of protein, and 9 grammes of fat.

Ingredients:

- 1 tablespoon extra-virgin olive oil
- 50 g butter (1.8 oz)
- 100 g (3.5 oz) milk chocolate chips
- four tbsp powdered sugar
- 2 eggs plus 2 yolks
- 1 tbsp. vanilla extract
- 4 tbsp unsweetened chocolate powder
- 100 g/3.5 oz unbleached flour
- 1 teaspoon sea salt
- 4 tablespoons of smooth peanut butter.

Method:

1. Preheat your air fryer to 150° Celsius (300° Fahrenheit) and line the bottom of the basket with parchment paper.
2. Lightly coat four small round ramekins with 1 teaspoon olive oil.
3. Melt the butter and chocolate chips in a microwave-safe dish in 30 second increments until completely melted.
4. Whisk in the powdered sugar, eggs, egg yolks, and vanilla extract until the mixture is smooth. Combine the cocoa powder, plain flour, and salt in a large mixing bowl.
5. Pour the mixture into the ramekins, filling them halfway. 1 tbsp of smooth peanut butter in each ramekin, followed by the remaining batter.
6. Wrap each ramekin in tin foil and place it in the air fryer basket.10–12 minutes in the oven.
7. Remove the tin foil from the top of each ramekin and continue to cook for 5 minutes.
8. Remove the ramekins from the air fryer and gently remove the cakes out of the ramekins, using a knife to run around the sides of the cakes.
9. Garnish with powdered sugar or an additional dollop of peanut butter while still hot.

Puff Pastry Cherry Pies in the Air Fryer

- This recipe serves 8 people.
- Preparation time: 15 minutes
- Time to cook: 10 minutes.

Nutritional information per serving: 298 calories, 27 grammes of carbohydrates, 8 grammes of protein, and 11 grammes of fat.

Ingredients:

- To make the puff pastry pies:
- Cherries (400 g, or 14 oz)
- 2 teaspoons stevia
- 1 teaspoon cornstarch
- 2 thawed puff pastry sheets.
- ONE EGG

To make the glaze:

- 2 tablespoons of heavy whipping cream.
- four tbsp powdered sugar
- 1/2 teaspoon almond extract
- 50 g (1.8 oz) flaked almonds

Method:

1. Preheat your air fryer to 180° Celsius (350°F) and line the bottom of the basket with parchment paper.
2. In a sauce pan over medium heat, heat the cherries for 3–4 minutes, or until they begin to exude water.2 tablespoons stevia, stirred in Reduce the heat to a low setting and continue to cook for 10 minutes.
3. In the meantime, make a paste with the corn starch and 1 tablespoon of water. Stir in the melted cherries and continue to cook for 2 minutes or until the sauce thickens. Take the pan off the heat and put it aside to cool.
4. Cut the puff pastry dough into even squares after rolling it out. Spoon the cherry filling into the Centre of each puff pastry square.
5. To cover the filling, fold the puff pastry dough diagonally. Seal the edges with a fork or by gently pinching them between your thumb and fingers.
6. Crack the egg into a mixing bowl and whisk thoroughly. Coat the tops of each pie with the egg using a pastry brush.
7. Cook the puff pastry cherry pies in the prepared air fryer basket for 10–12 minutes, or until golden brown.
8. Meanwhile, create the glaze by combining the heavy whipping cream, powdered sugar, and almond extract in a mixing dish.
9. Remove the puff pastry cherry pies from the air fryer and set them aside to cool on a cooling rack.
10. Once the pies have cooled, drizzle them with part of the glaze and sprinkle with flaked almonds.

11. Serve the cherry pies warm or cold, with whipped cream on the side.

Chocolate Donuts in the Air Fryer

- This recipe serves 4 people.
- 1 hour and 20 minutes to prepare.
- Time to cook: 10 minutes.

Nutritional data per serving: 355 calories, 42 grammes of carbohydrates, 10 grammes of protein, and 15 grammes of fat.

Ingredients:

Regarding the donuts:

- Milk (200 mL)
- 100 g sugar (3.5 oz)
- 2 teaspoons of active dry yeast (1 packet)
- 4 tablespoons melted butter
- ONE EGG
- 1 tbsp. vanilla extract
- (400 g/14 oz) plain flour
- Four tbsp cocoa powder

To make the icing:

- 6 tablespoons of powdered sugar.
- 2 tbsp unsweetened chocolate powder
- 100 mL heavy cream
- chopped mixed nuts,(1.8 oz/50 g)

Method:

1. In a mixing bowl, combine the milk, sugar, and yeast to create the doughnuts. Set it aside and wait for the yeast to bubble up.
2. Stir in the melted butter, egg, and vanilla extract until thoroughly combined.
3. Stir in the plain flour and unsweetened cocoa powder. Mix until the mixture is smooth.
4. Flour a clean surface lightly, and roll out the dough on top. Knead the dough for 2-3 minutes, or until it is soft and somewhat sticky.
5. Place the dough in a large mixing bowl, cover with a clean tea towel, and set aside in a warm place for one hour to rise.
6. After one hour, put some flour on a clean surface and spread out the dough to a thickness of about half an inch.
7. Using a round cookie cutter, cut out small round donuts.Place the doughnuts in the air fryer. Preheat the air fryer but do not oil the basket.
8. Preheat the air fryer to 150 °C (300 °F) and close the lid. Cook the donuts for 8–10 minutes, or until the outsides are set but the insides are slightly soft. Set it aside while you prepare the frosting.

9. In a mixing bowl, combine the powdered sugar, unsweetened cocoa powder, and heavy cream to create the icing. Mix well until a smooth, sticky mixture is formed.
10. Cover the top of each doughnut with frosting using an icing pipe or a spoon. Sprinkle chopped mixed nuts on top of each doughnut.
11. As a dessert, serve the doughnuts warm or cold.

Biscuits in the Air Fryer

- This recipe serves 8 people.
- Preparation time: 15 minutes
- Time to cook-10 minutes

Nutritional data per serving: 134 calories, 12 grammes of carbohydrates, 2 grammes of protein, and 8 grammes of fat.

Ingredients:

- (400 g/14 oz) plain flour
- 2 teaspoons baking powder
- 1 teaspoon sugar
- 1/2 teaspoon of salt
- 50 g butter (1.8 oz)
- Cashew milk, 200 mL

Method:

1. Preheat your air fryer to 200° Celsius (400° Fahrenheit) and line the bottom of the basket with parchment paper.
2. Combine the plain flour and butter in a large mixing basin. Mix well to make a crumb-like substance.
3. Combine the baking powder, sugar, and salt in a mixing bowl. 5. Mix well before adding the cashew milk. Combine all of the ingredients until they create smooth dough.
4. On a lightly floured surface, roll out the dough. Cut tiny, round biscuits from the dough using a biscuit cutter.
5. Place the biscuits in the air fryer basket and shut the machine's lid. 10 minutes, or until golden and crispy.
6. Serve warm or chilled.

Air Fryer Chocolate Brownies

- This recipe serves 4 people.
- Preparation time: 5 minutes
- 15 minutes of cooking time.

Nutritional data per serving: 189 calories, 12 grammes of carbohydrates, 4 grammes of protein, and 9 grammes of fat.

Ingredients:

- 100 g (3.5 oz) granulated sugar
- 8 teaspoon cocoa powder
- 100 g/3.5 oz unbleached flour
- 1/2 teaspoons of baking powder
- 1/2 teaspoon of salt
- Melted butter. 50 g/1.8 oz.
- ONE EGG

Method:

1. Preheat your air fryer to 180° Celsius (350°F) and line the bottom of the basket with parchment paper.
2. Combine the sugar, cocoa powder, plain flour, baking powder, and salt in a mixing dish. Combine thoroughly.
3. Add the melted butter and the egg to the bowl. Whisk until all of the ingredients are well blended.
4. Pour the brownie batter into the air fryer basket that has been prepared. Cook for 15 minutes, or until the top is set but the Centre is still somewhat soft.
5. Take the brownies out of the air fryer and set them aside to cool before cutting them into four portions.
6. Serve with ice cream or whipped cream, hot or cold.

Lava Cake in the Air Fryer

- This recipe serves 4 people.
- Preparation time: 5 minutes
- Time to cook: 10 minutes.

Nutritional data per serving: 359 calories, 19 grammes of carbohydrates, 6 grammes of protein, and 15 grammes of fat.

Ingredients:

- 100 g (3.5 oz) milk chocolate chips
- 5 tablespoons cubed butter
- 100 g sugar (3.5 oz)
- Two large eggs and two yolks
- 1 tablespoon extract of peppermint
- 100 g/3.5 oz unbleached flour

Method:

1. Preheat your air fryer to 180° Celsius (350°F) and line the bottom of the basket with parchment paper.
2. In a large heatproof dish, combine the milk chocolate chips and butter and microwave in 30 second increments until completely melted. Stir well in between intervals.
3. Combine the sugar, eggs, egg yolks, and peppermint essence in a mixing bowl. Combine thoroughly.
4. Stir in the flour and continue to mix until all of the ingredients are blended.
5. Place the cake batter in the preheated air fryer basket and shut the machine's lid. Cook for 10–12 minutes, or until the surface is set but the Centre is still soft.
6. Remove the cake from the air fryer and set aside for 5 minutes before slicing.
7. Serve it hot or cold, with ice cream or whipped cream on the side.

BONUS POULTRY RECIPES

Wings of Korean Chicken

- 2 servings
- 356 calories, 23 g protein, 26 g fat, and 6 g carbohydrates.

INGREDIENTS:

- 1 kilogramme of chicken wings (bones included).
- 1 teaspoon sea salt
- 1 teaspoon ground black pepper
- 2 tablespoons Gochujang
- 1 teaspoon of mayonnaise
- 1 teaspoon of agave nectar
- 1 tbsp sesame seed oil
- 1 tablespoon minced ginger
- 1 tbsp. minced garlic
- Two Splenda packets

DIRECTIONS:

1. Preheat the air fryer to 200° Celsius.
2. Line a small baking dish with foil.
3. Season the chicken wings with salt and pepper before placing them in the pan and putting them in the air fryer.
4. Bake for 20 minutes, flipping halfway through.
5. In a medium mixing bowl, add the remaining sauce ingredients.
6. Coat the chicken wings with the sauce, mixing well.
7. Continue to cook for 5 minutes in the air fryer.

Tandoori Chicken is delicious

- 2 servings
- 178 calories, 25g protein, 6g fat, and 2g carbohydrates

INGREDIENTS:

- 500g chicken tenders, cut in half
- 75g Greek plain yoghurt
- 1 tablespoon minced ginger
- 1 tbsp. minced garlic
- 1 paprika teaspoon
- 1 teaspoon sea salt
- Cayenne pepper 1 teaspoon
- 1 tsp. garam masala
- 1 tablespoon turmeric
- 1/2 cups of cilantro, chopped

DIRECTIONS:

1. In a large mixing bowl, combine all of the ingredients except the chicken.
2. Preheat the air fryer to 160° Celsius.
3. Place the chicken in the air fryer and drizzle with oil.
4. Cook for 10 minutes before flipping and cooking for another 5 minutes.
5. Pour the sauce over the chicken and continue to cook for 5 minutes.
6. Present!

Jalfrezi Chicken

- 4 servings
- 247 calories, 23 grammes of protein, 12 grammes of fat, and 9 grammes of carbohydrates

INGREDIENTS:

- 500g of chicken, bones and skin removed.
- 1 onion, chopped
- 2 chopped bell peppers.
- 4 tablespoons of tomato sauce.
- 1 teaspoon of water
- 2 tablespoons of olive oil.
- 1 teaspoon sea salt
- 2 tablespoons garam masala
- 1 tablespoon turmeric
- cayenne pepper 1 teaspoon

DIRECTIONS:

1. Combine the oil, chicken, onions, pepper, salt, half of the garam masala, turmeric, and half of the cayenne pepper in a large mixing bowl.
2. Cook for 15 minutes at 180 degrees Celsius in an air fryer.
3. In a medium mixing bowl (microwave safe), combine the tomato sauce, water, salt, remaining garam masala, and cayenne pepper.
4. Cook for 1 minute in the microwave, then stir and cook for another minute.
5. Take the chicken out of the air fryer and drizzle with the sauce.
6. Serve right away with hot rice.

Burgers with turkey and mushrooms

- 2 servings
- 132 calories, 25g protein, 26g fat, and 25g carbohydrates

INGREDIENTS:

- 180 gram(s) mushrooms
- 500g minced turkey
- 1 tablespoon garlic powder
- 1 tsp. onion powder
- 1/2 teaspoon salt
- 1/2 teaspoon pepper

DIRECTIONS:

1. Place the mushrooms in a food processor and pulse until they create a puree. Season and pulse once more.
2. Remove from the food processor and place in a mixing bowl.
3. Fold in the turkey until well combined.
4. Form burgers using a small amount of the ingredients in your palms. You should be able to create five of them.
5. Spray each burger lightly with cooking spray and place it in the air fryer.
6. Bake for 10 minutes at 160 degrees Celsius.

Tender Chicken Tenders

- 4 servings
- 253 calories, 26.2g protein, 11.4g fat, and 9.8g carbohydrates

INGREDIENTS:

- ONE EGG
- 2 tablespoons of olive oil.
- 50 grammes bread crumbs
- 8 pieces of chicken tenders (frozen)

DIRECTIONS:

1. Preheat the fryer to 175 degrees Celsius.
2. In a small bowl, beat the egg.
3. Combine the oil and bread crumbs in a separate dish.
4. Dip one tender first in the egg, then in the breadcrumbs.
5. Put the tender into the frying basket.
6. Repeat with the rest of the tenders, being careful not to overlap them.
7. Allow 12 minutes to cook before serving!

Chicken Nuggets in a Hurry

- 4 servings
- 244 calories, 31 grammes of protein, 3.6 grammes of fat, and 25 grammes of carbohydrates

INGREDIENTS:

- Chicken tenders, 500g
- 4 tbsp. salad dressing mix
- 2 tablespoons of plain flour.
- 1 egg, beaten
- 50 grammes bread crumbs

DIRECTIONS:

1. Place the chicken in a large mixing dish.
2. Sprinkle the seasoning evenly over the top of the chicken.
3. Set aside the chicken for 10 minutes to rest.
4. Place the flour in a sealable bag.
5. Place the breadcrumbs on a medium platter.
6. Place the chicken in a resalable bag and shake to coat with the flour.
7. Remove the chicken from the pan and coat it evenly with breadcrumbs.
8. Do the same with the chicken.
9. Preheat the air fryer to 200 degrees Celsius.
10. Place the chicken in the fryer for 4 minutes before flipping and cooking for another 4 minutes.
11. Remove from the oven and serve immediately.

Chicken Thighs Wrapped in Bacon

- 4 servings
- 453 calories, 34g fat, 150g protein, and 33g carbohydrates

INGREDIENTS:

- 150g of softened butter.
- 1 garlic clove, minced
- 1/4 teaspoon of dried thyme
- 1/4 tsp. basil (dried)
- A grain of salt
- A pinch of black pepper
- Five bacon rashers
- 5 chicken thighs, skin and bones removed.

DIRECTIONS:

1. In a mixing bowl, combine the melted butter, garlic, thyme, basil, salt, and pepper.
2. Roll up the cling film with the butter. Refrigerate for at least one hour before serving.
3. Two hours
4. Place one piece of bacon on top of the butter to coat it slightly.
5. Arrange the chicken thighs over the bacon.
6. Garnish with a little more garlic
7. Place a little amount of butter in the center of the chicken thigh and tuck the end of the bacon into the chicken to secure it.
8. Preheat the air fryer to 180° Celsius.
9. Cook the chicken until it is white in the center.

Chicken Wings with Buffalo Sauce

- 4 servings
- 481 calories, 41g fat, 20g protein, and 7g carbohydrates

INGREDIENTS:

- 500g chicken wings
- 1 tablespoon extra-virgin olive oil
- 1 tbsp. cayenne pepper
- 150g of softened butter.
- 2 tablespoons of vinegar.
- 1 tablespoon garlic powder

DIRECTIONS:

1. Preheat the air fryer to 180° Celsius.
2. Place the chicken in a large mixing dish.
3. Drizzle the oil evenly over the wings.
4. Cook the wings for 25 minutes, then turn them and cook for another 5 minutes.
5. Melt the butter, vinegar, garlic powder, and cayenne pepper in a medium saucepan over medium heat.
6. Pour the sauce over the wings and toss to coat.
7. Present!

BONUS SEAFOOD DISHES

Fillets of tilapia

- 2 servings
- 724 calories, 41 grammes of protein, 59 grammes of fat, and 13 grammes of carbohydrates

INGREDIENTS:

- 50 grammes of almond flour.
- 2 fillets of tilapia
- 2 tbsp. softened butter
- 1 teaspoon ground black pepper
- 1/2 teaspoon salt
- 4 teaspoons mayonnaise
- A handful of finely sliced almonds

DIRECTIONS:

1. In a mixing dish, combine the almond flour, butter, pepper, and salt.
2. Spread the mayonnaise on both sides of the fish.
3. Coat the fillets with the almond flour mixture.
4. Spread the chopped almonds on one side of the fish.
5. Coat the air fryer with cooking spray.
6. Cook the fish in the air fryer for 10 minutes at 160 oC.

Crispy fish

- 4 servings
- 354 calories, 26.9g of protein, 17.7g of fat, and 22.5g of carbohydrates.

INGREDIENTS:

- 100 gramme (dry) breadcrumbs
- 1/4 cup extra virgin olive oil
- 4 fillets of your preferred fish.
- 1 egg, beaten
- 1 lemon, sliced

DIRECTIONS:

1. Preheat the oven to 180° Celsius.
2. Combine the olive oil and breadcrumbs in a medium mixing basin.
3. Dip the fish into the egg, then into the breadcrumbs, ensuring it is equally covered.
4. Place the fish in the basket.
5. 5 minutes in the oven
6. Remove from the oven and serve immediately with lemon slices.

Shrimp with Honey and Garlic (Gluten-Free)

- 2 servings
- 486 calories, 25 grammes of protein, 26 grammes of fat, and 25 grammes of carbohydrates

INGREDIENTS:

- 1/2 cup of honey.
- Fresh shrimp 450g
- 1/2 cup gluten-free soy sauce
- 2 tablespoons (tomato ketchup)
- 1 package frozen stir fry vegetables
- 1 garlic clove, mashed
- 1 tsp. fresh ginger
- 2 teaspoons corn starch

DIRECTIONS:

1. In a medium saucepan over medium heat, combine the honey, soy sauce, garlic, tomato ketchup, and ginger.
2. Continue to stir in the corn starch until the sauce thickens.
3. Drizzle the sauce over the shrimp.
4. Line the interior of the air fryer with foil and place the shrimp and veggies inside.
5. Bake for 10 minutes at 180 degrees Celsius.

Fish Tacos on the Air Fryer

- 4 servings
- 486 calories, 25 grammes of protein, 26 grammes of fat, and 25 grammes of carbohydrates

INGREDIENTS:

- 500g fresh mahi
- 8 small tortillas
- 2 tsp. Cajun seasoning
- 4 tbsp. soured cream
- 2 tablespoons mayonnaise
- 1/4 teaspoons of cayenne pepper
- 2 teaspoons pepper sauce
- A pinch of salt and pepper.
- 1 tbsp. Sriracha sauce
- 2 teaspoons lime juice

DIRECTIONS:

1. Season the fish with salt and pepper.
2. Combine the cayenne pepper, black pepper, and Cajun seasoning in a mixing bowl. Drizzling on fish
3. Brush the fish on both sides with the pepper sauce.
4. Heat the air fryer to 180 degrees Celsius and cook for 10 minutes.
5. In a medium mixing bowl, combine the mayonnaise, sour cream, lime juice, sriracha, and cayenne pepper.
6. Assemble and serve the tacos!

Shrimp with Yum Yum sauce

- 4 servings
- 486 calories, 25 grammes of protein, 34 grammes of fat, and 25 grammes of carbohydrates

INGREDIENTS:

- 500g jumbo peeled shrimp
- 1 teaspoon of soy sauce
- 1 teaspoon garlic paste
- 1 teaspoon ginger paste
- One-quarter cup mayonnaise
- 1/4 cups of ketchup (tomato)
- 1 paprika teaspoon
- 1 teaspoon sugar
- 1 tablespoon garlic powder

DIRECTIONS:

1. Combine the soy sauce, garlic paste, and ginger paste in a mixing bowl.
2. Marinate the shrimp in the basin for 15 minutes.
3. To prepare the sauce, mix the ketchup, mayonnaise, sugar, paprika, and garlic powder in a separate bowl.
4. Preheat the air fryer to 200 degrees Celsius.
5. Cook the shrimp for 8–10 minutes in the basket.
6. When finished, add the sauce and thoroughly combine.

Shrimp Cajun Style

- 6 servings
- 340 calories, 30 grammes of protein, 26 grammes of fat, and 22 grammes of carbohydrates

INGREDIENTS:

- 250 grammes cooked shrimp
- 14 slices smoked sausage
- 4 cups parboiled potatoes, halved
- 2 cobs of corn split into smaller pieces.
- 1 onion, diced
- 2 teaspoons bay seasoning

DIRECTIONS:

1. In a mixing bowl, combine all of the ingredients and thoroughly mix them together.
2. Prepare the air fryer by lining it with aluminium foil.
3. Cook for 6 minutes at 200 oC in the air fryer with half of the mixture.
4. Recombine everything and cook for 6 minutes more.
5. Continue with the second batch.
6. Present!

Salmon with Sriracha

- 2 servings
- 320 calories, 25 grammes of protein, 34 grammes of fat, and 25 grammes of carbohydrates.

INGREDIENTS:

- 3 tablespoons Sriracha
- Four tablespoons honey
- 1 teaspoon of soy sauce
- 500g salmon fillets

DIRECTIONS:

1. In a medium mixing bowl, combine the honey, soy sauce, and sriracha.
2. Place the salmon skin-side up in the sauce.
3. Set aside for 30 minutes to marinate.
4. Lightly coat the air fryer basket with cooking spray.
5. Preheat the air fryer to 200° Celsius.
6. Cook the salmon for 12 minutes in the air fryer, skin side down.
7. Present!

BONUS VEGETABLE DISHES

Burgers with falafel

- 2 servings
- 709 calories, 30 grammes of protein, 26 grammes of fat, and 92 grammes of carbohydrates

INGREDIENTS:

- 400g canned chickpeas
- 1 sliced small onion
- 1 lime
- oats (140 g)
- 28g of cheese.
- feta cheese (28g)
- Seasoned with salt and pepper.
- 2 teaspoons Greek yoghurt
- 4 tablespoons of soft cheese.
- 1 tablespoon puréed garlic
- 1 tablespoon cilantro
- 1 tablespoon dried oregano
- 1 tbsp. chopped parsley

DIRECTIONS:

1. Combine the chickpeas, onion, lemon rind, garlic, and spices in a blender. 2. Blend until coarse.
2. Pour half of the soft cheese, cheese, and feta into a mixing bowl.
3. Form into burgers and top with oats.
4. In an air fryer, cook for 8 minutes at 180°C.
5. In a mixing dish, combine the remaining soft cheese, Greek yoghurt, and lemon juice to form the sauce.
6. When the burgers are done, cover them with the sauce.

Burgers with lentils

- 4 servings
- 509 calories, 21 grammes of protein, 8 grammes of fat, and 90 grammes of carbohydrates

INGREDIENTS:

- 100g black buluga lentils
- 1 carrot, grated
- 1 onion, diced
- 100g white cabbage, sliced
- Oats 300g
- 1 tablespoon puréed garlic
- 1 tablespoon cumin
- Salt
- Pepper

DIRECTIONS:

1. Blend the oats until they are the consistency of flour.
2. Place the lentils in a pot. Cook for 45 minutes after adding some water.
3. Steam the veggies for 5 minutes, or until they are tender.
4. Combine all of the ingredients in a mixing basin.
5. Using your hands, shape the mixture into patties.
6. Cook for 30 minutes at 180 o C in an air fryer.

Burgers with Zucchini

- 4 servings
- 36 calories, 3 g protein, 1 g fat, and 6 g carbohydrates.

INGREDIENTS:

- 1 courgette
- 1 small can chickpeas, drained
- 3 spring onions, chopped
- A smidgeon of dried garlic
- Salt
- Pepper
- 3 tbsp fresh coriander
- 1 tsp. chilli powder
- 1 tsp mixed spices
- 1 tablespoon cumin

DIRECTIONS:

1. In a large mixing bowl, grate the zucchini, discarding any extra water.
2. Combine the spring onions, chickpeas, zucchini, and spice in a mixing bowl.
3. Using your hands, bind the ingredients together into burgers.
4. In an air fryer, cook for 12 minutes at 200°C.

Meatballs made with zucchini

- 4 servings
- 203 calories, 9g protein, 6g fat, and 29g carbohydrates

INGREDIENTS:

- 150g oatmeal
- 40g feta crumble
- One beaten egg
- Seasoned with salt and pepper.
- 150 gramme zucchini
- 1 tsp. lemon rind
- Six finely cut basil leaves
- 1 teaspoon fresh dill
- 1 teaspoon dried oregano

DIRECTIONS:

1. Preheat the air fryer to 200° Celsius.
2. Squeeze off any extra water after grating the zucchini into a basin.
3. Stir in the other ingredients, except the oats.
4. In a blender, grind the oats until they resemble breadcrumbs.
5. 5. Combine everything in the bowl, including the oats.
6. Roll the mixture into balls and cook in an air fryer.
7. Bake for 10 minutes.

Quiche with Macaroni and Cheese

- 4 servings
- 191 calories, 10 grammes of protein, 8 grammes of fat, and 18 grammes of carbohydrates

INGREDIENTS:

- 8 tablespoons of macaroni cheese
- 2-shortcrust pastry sheets
- 2 teaspoons Greek yoghurt
- Two eggs
- Milk (150 ml)
- 1 teaspoon puréed garlic
- To serve, sprinkle with grated cheese.

DIRECTIONS:

1. Dust the insides of four ramekins with flour.
2. Use the pastry to line the ramekins.
3. In a mixing dish, combine the yoghurt, garlic, and macaroni.
4. Spoon the mixture into the ramekins until they are 3/4 full.
5. Whisk together the egg and milk then pour over the macaroni before topping with the cheese.
6. Heat the air fryer to 180°C and cook for 20 minutes, or until golden brown.

Gratin de pommes

- 4 servings
- 232 calories, 9 grammes of protein, 15 grammes of fat, and 16 grammes of carbohydrates

INGREDIENTS:

- 2 large potatoes
- Two beaten eggs
- 1 gallon coconut cream
- 1 tbsp unbleached flour
- 50g of cheddar cheese, grated

DIRECTIONS:

1. Thinly slice the potatoes and throw them in the air fryer.
2. Bake for 10 minutes at 180°C.
3. Combine the eggs, coconut cream, and flour in a large mixing basin. 4.
4. Arrange the potato pieces in four ramekins.
5. Spread the cream mixture over the top and sprinkle with the cheese.
6. Bake for 10 minutes at 200°C.

BONUS BEEF RECIPES

Wraps filled with meatloaf

Preparation time: 15 minutes

Time to cook: 10 minutes.

2 servings

Ingredients:

- 1 pound ground grass-fed beef
- ½ cup of almond flour
- ¼ cup of coconut flour
- ½ tablespoon minced garlic
- 1/4 cup white onion, finely sliced
- 1 teaspoon of Italian seasoning
- ½ teaspoon of sea salt
- ½ teaspoon tarragon dried
- ½ teaspoon black pepper, ground
- 1 tablespoon of Worcestershire sauce.
- Ketchup, 1/4 cup
- 2 pastured eggs, beaten
- 1 head lettuce

Directions:

1. Toss all of the ingredients together in a mixing bowl, then shape into 2-inch diameter and 1-inch thick patties and chill for 10 minutes.
2. In the meantime, turn on the air fryer, insert the frying basket, coat it with olive oil, close the cover, and warm it for 10 minutes at 360 o F.
3. Preheat the fryer, place the patties in a single layer, shut the lid, and cook for 10 minutes, or until pleasantly browned and done, turning halfway through the cooking.
4. When the air fryer sounds, remove the patties and place them on a platter.
5. Wrap each patty in lettuce and serve.

Nutrition:

- 228 calories
- 6 g carbohydrate
- Fat: 16 g
- 13 grammes of protein
- 2 g dietary fibre

A burger with two cheeses

Preparation time: 5 minutes

Time to cook: 18 minutes.

1 serving

Ingredients:

- Two pastured beef patties.
- 1/8 tablespoon onion powder
- 2 low-fat mozzarella cheese slices
- 1/8 teaspoon ground black pepper
- a quarter teaspoon of salt
- 2 tablespoons of olive oil.

Directions:

1. Preheat the air fryer to 370oF for 5 minutes, insert the basket, coat with olive oil, and close the cover.
2. In the meantime, season the patties well with onion powder, black pepper, and salt.
3. Preheat the fryer, add the beef patties, close the lid, and cook for 12 minutes, or until the patties are pleasantly browned and done, rotating halfway through.
4. Top each patty with a cheese slice and heat for 1 minute, or until the cheese melts.
5. Serve right away.

Nutrition:

- 670 calories
- 0 g carbohydrates
- Fat: 50 g
- 39 grammes of protein
- 0 g fibre

Schnitzel (beef)

Preparation time: 10 minutes

Time to cook: 15 minutes.

1 serving

Ingredients:

- 1 lean meat schnitzel
- 2 tablespoons of olive oil.
- ¼ cup of bread crumbs
- 1 egg
- To serve, 1 lemon and salad greens.

Directions:

1. Preheat the air fryer to 180 degrees Celsius.
2. In a large mixing bowl, combine breadcrumbs and oil and stir thoroughly until a crumbly mixture forms.
3. After dipping the beef steak in the whisked egg, coat it in the breadcrumb mixture.
4. Cook the breaded beef in the air fryer for 15 minutes or longer, or until thoroughly cooked through.
5. Remove from the air fryer and serve immediately with salad leaves and lemon wedges on the side.

Nutrition:

- 340 calories
- Protein (20 g)
- 14 g carbohydrates
- Fat: 10 g
- 7 grammes of fibre

Bundles of steak with asparagus

Time to prepare: 20 minutes.

Time to cook: 30 minutes.

2 servings

Ingredients:

- Spray with olive oil.
- 6, 2 pound flank steak slices
- Black pepper with kosher salt.
- 2 minced garlic cloves.
- Four cups of asparagus
- Tamari sauce, 1/2 teaspoon
- 3 finely sliced bell peppers.
- 1/3 cup beef broth
- 1 tbsp. unsalted butter
- ¼ cup of balsamic vinegar

Directions:

1. Season and massage the meat with salt and pepper.
2. In a Ziploc bag, combine the garlic and Tamari sauce, then add the steak, stir well, and seal the bag.
3. Marinate it for 1 hour or overnight.
4. Distribute the bell peppers and asparagus evenly over the middle of the steak.
5. Tightly wrap the steak around the vegetables and secure with toothpicks.

6. Preheat the air fryer to high.
7. Spray the steak with olive oil. Place the steaks in the air fryer.
8. Cook for 15 minutes at 400 degrees Fahrenheit, or until the steaks are done.
9. Remove the steak from the air fryer and set it aside to rest for 5 minutes.
10. Remove the steak bundles and set them aside for 5 minutes before serving and slicing.
11. Meanwhile, heat the butter, balsamic vinegar, and broth over medium heat. Cut in half after thoroughly mixing. Season with salt and pepper to taste.
12. Drizzle over steaks just before serving.

Nutrition:

- 471 calories
- Protein content: 29 g
- 20 g carbohydrates
- Fat: 15 g

Hamburgers

Preparation time: 5 minutes

Time to cook: 6 minutes.

4 servings

Ingredients:

- 4 buns
- 4 cups lean ground beef chuck
- Season with salt to taste.
- 4 slivers of any cheese.
- Black pepper to taste
- 2 cut tomatoes
- 1 head lettuce
- Using ketchup as a dressing

Directions:

1. Preheat the air fryer to 350 degrees Fahrenheit.
2. In a mixing bowl, combine lean ground beef, pepper, and salt. Form patties from the mixture.
3. Cook for 6 minutes, flipping halfway through, in a single layer in the air fryer. For 1 minute before removing the patties, sprinkle with cheese.
4. Remove the cheese from the air fryer after it has melted.
5. Spread ketchup or other dressing on your buns; top with tomatoes, lettuce, and patties.
6. Serve right away.

Nutrition:

- 520 calories
- Carbohydrates: 22 g.
- Protein: 31 g
- Fat, 34 g

Kabobs of Beef Steak with Vegetables

Preparation time: 30 minutes

Time to cook: 10 minutes.

4 servings

Ingredients:

- 2 tbsp soy sauce (light)
- 4 cups lean beef chuck ribs, cut up
- 1/3 cup low-fat sour cream
- 1/2 onion
- 8 skewers, 6 in.
- 1 small red bell pepper
- Pepper, black
- Dupable yoghurt

Directions:

1. Combine soy sauce and sour cream in a mixing basin. Add the lean beef pieces, coat thoroughly, and marinate for 30 minutes or longer.
2. Cube the onion and bell pepper. Soak skewers in water for 10 minutes.
3. Skewer the onions, bell peppers, and meat; season with black pepper if desired.
4. Cook for 10 minutes in a preheated air fryer at 400 o F, flipping halfway through.
5. Serve with the yoghurt dipping sauce.

Nutrition:

- 268 calories
- Protein (20 g)
- 15 g carbohydrate
- Fat: 10 g

Steak Rib-Eye

Preparation time: 5 minutes

Time to cook: 14 minutes.

2 servings

Ingredients:

- 2 medium-sized lean ribeye steaks.
- To -taste, season with salt and freshly ground black pepper.
- Salad with micro greens to serve

Directions:

1. Preheat the air fryer to 400 degrees Fahrenheit. Using paper towels, pat dry the steaks.
2. Season steaks with any spice mixture or simply salt and pepper.
3. Apply it liberally to both sides of the meat.
4. Place steaks in the air fryer basket. Cook to the desired level of rareness. Alternatively, cook for 14 minutes and flip after half.
5. Remove from the air fryer and place on a cooling rack for 5 minutes.
6. Serve with a micro green salad.

Nutrition:

- 470 calories
- 45 grammes of protein
- Fat: 31 g
- 23 g carbohydrate

Sloppy Joes without meat

Preparation time: 15 minutes

Time to cook: 40 minutes.

2 servings

Ingredients:

- 6 large sweet potatoes
- 1 pound (454 g) lean ground beef
- 1 onion, finely chopped
- 1 carrot, finely sliced
- 1/4 cup finely chopped mushrooms
- 1/4 cup finely chopped red bell pepper
- 3 garlic cloves, minced
- 2 tbsp. Worcestershire sauce

- 1 tablespoon of white wine vinegar.
- 1 low-sodium tomato sauce cans (15 oz/425 g)
- Two tbsp tomato paste

Directions:

1. Preheat the air fryer oven to 400 degrees Fahrenheit (205 degrees Celsius).
2. Arrange the sweet potatoes in a single layer in a baking dish. Bake for 25–40 minutes (depending on size), or until tender and cooked through.
3. While the sweet potatoes are roasting, brown the meat in a large pan over medium heat, breaking it up into tiny pieces as you stir.
4. Sauté the onion, carrot, mushrooms, bell pepper, and garlic for 1 minute.
5. Combine the Worcestershire sauce, vinegar, tomato sauce, and tomato paste in a mixing bowl. Bring to a simmer, and then lower to a low heat for 5 minutes to let the flavours mingle.
6. To serve, spoon 1/2 cups of the beef mixture on top of each cooked potato.

Nutrition:

- 372 calories
- Fat: 19 g
- Protein (16 g)
- Carbohydrates: 34 g
- 13 grammes of sugar
- 6 g fibre
- 161 milligrams of sodium

"Curry with Beef"

Preparation time: 15 minutes

Time to cook: 10 minutes.

2 servings

Ingredients:

- 1 tablespoon olive oil (extra virgin)
- 1 tiny onion, finely sliced
- 2 tsp of fresh ginger, minced
- 3 garlic cloves, minced
- 2 teaspoons of ground coriander.
- 1 tsp. cumin powder
- 1 Serrano or jalapeo pepper, cut lengthwise but not through
- All the way through
- A quarter teaspoon turmeric powder
- A quarter teaspoon of salt

- Grass-fed sirloin tip steak, top round steak, or top round steak 1 pound (454 g)
- Cut sirloin steak into bite-size chunks.
- 2 tbsp. fresh cilantro, chopped
- 1/4 cups of water

Directions:

1. In an air fryer oven, heat the oil to medium-high.
2. Cook for 3 to 5 minutes, or until the onion is softened and caramelized. Stir in the ginger and garlic for approximately 30 seconds, or until fragrant.
3. Combine the coriander, cumin, jalapeo, turmeric, and salt in a small bowl.
4. Stir continually for 1 minute after adding the spice combination to the skillet. 1/4 cups of water should be used to deglaze the skillet.
5. Cook for about 5 minutes, stirring constantly, until the beef is well-browned but still medium-rare. Take out the jalapeo. Garnish with cilantro and serve.

Nutrition:

- 140 calories
- Fat: 7 g
- Protein content: 18 g
- 3 g carbohydrate
- 1 grammes sugar
- 1 grammes of fibre
- 141 milligrams of sodium

Salad with Asian Grilled Beef

Preparation time: 15 minutes

Time to cook: 15 minutes.

4 servings

Ingredients:

Dressing:

- 1/4 cup freshly squeezed lime juice
- 1 tbsp gluten-free soy sauce or tamari with low sodium
- 1 tablespoon olive oil (extra virgin)
- 1 garlic clove, minced
- 1 tablespoon honey
- 1/4 teaspoons of red pepper flakes

Salad:

- 1 pound grass-fed flank steak (454 g)
- a quarter teaspoon of salt

- 1 teaspoon black pepper, freshly ground
- 6 cups of leaf lettuce, chopped
- Sliced into half-moons after being halved lengthwise
- 1 small chopped red onion
- 1 carrot, snipped into ribbons
- 1/4 cup fresh cilantro, chopped

Directions:

Prepare the salad:

- Whisk together the lime juice, tamari, olive oil, garlic, honey, and red pepper flakes in a small bowl. Place aside.

Prepare the Salad:

1. Season both sides of the meat with salt and pepper.
2. Preheat the air fryer to 400 degrees Fahrenheit (205 degrees Celsius).
3. Cook the beef for 3 to 6 minutes on each side, depending on how well done you want it. Set aside for 10 minutes, tented with aluminium foil.
4. Toss the lettuce, cucumber, onion, carrot, and cilantro in a large mixing dish.
5. Thinly slice the meat against the grain and place it in the salad dish.
6. Drizzle with the dressing and mix well. Serve

Nutrition:

- 231 calories
- Fat: 10 g
- Protein content: 26 g
- 10 g carbohydrate
- 4 g of sugar
- 2 g dietary fibre
- 349 milligrams sodium

Pot Roast on Sunday

Preparation time: 10 minutes

Cooking time is 1 hour 45 minutes.

4 servings

Ingredients:

- 1 beef rump roast (3-4 pounds/1.4-1.8 kilograms)
- 2 tbsp. kosher salt, divided
- 2 tablespoons of avocado oil.
- 1 big onion, finely chopped (about 112 cups).
- 4 big carrots, chopped into 4 pieces each.

- 1 tbsp. minced garlic
- 3 cups of beef broth (low sodium)
- 1 teaspoon freshly ground black pepper
- 1 tbsp. dried parsley
- 2 tablespoons of all-purpose flour

Directions:

1. Sprinkle 1 teaspoon salt over the roast.
2. Preheat the air fryer to 400 degrees Fahrenheit (205 degrees Celsius).
3. Add the avocado oil. Place the roast in the saucepan with care and sear it for 6 to 9 minutes on each side. (A dark caramelised crust is desired.) Click "Cancel."
4. Remove the roast from the cooker and place it on a dish.
5. Add the onion, carrots, and garlic to the saucepan in that order.
6. Place the roast on top of the veggies, along with any liquid that has gathered.
7. Combine the broth, remaining 1 teaspoon salt, pepper, and parsley in a medium mixing bowl. Over the roast, pour the broth mixture.
8. Close and lock the air fryer's cover. Set the valve to the sealing position.
9. Cook on high pressure for 1 hour and 30 minutes.
10. When the cooking is finished, press "Cancel" and let the pressure drop normally.
11. When the pin falls, release and remove the lid.
12. Transfer the roast and vegetables to a serving plate using big slotted spoons while you create the gravy.
13. Remove the fat from the liquids in the saucepan using a big spoon or a fat separator. Bring the liquid to a boil in the electric pressure cooker on the "Sauté" setting.
14. To form slurry, mix together the flour and 4 tablespoons of water in a small bowl. Pour the slurry into the saucepan and whisk periodically until the gravy reaches the desired thickness. Season with salt and pepper to taste.
15. Toss the meat and carrots with the gravy and serve.

Nutrition:

- 245 calories
- Fat: 10 g
- Protein content: 33 g
- 6 g carbohydrate
- 2 g of sugar
- 1 grammes of fibre
- 397 mg/s...

Fajita Bowls with Beef and Peppers

Preparation time: 10 minutes

Time to cook: 15 minutes.

4 servings

Ingredients:

- 4 tbsp extra virgin olive oil
- 1 riced cauliflower head
- 1 pound (454 g) cut into 14-inch strips sirloin steak
- 1 red bell pepper, seeded and sliced
- 1 onion, finely sliced
- 2 minced garlic cloves.
- 2 squeezed limes
- 1 tsp. chilli powder

Directions:

1. Preheat the air fryer oven to 400 degrees Fahrenheit (205 degrees Celsius).
2. Heat 2 tablespoons olive oil in a small saucepan over medium heat until it shimmers.
3. Stir in the cauliflower." Cook, stirring periodically, for 3 minutes, or until it softens. Place aside.
4. Heat the remaining 2 tablespoons of oil in the air fryer on medium-high until it shimmers.
5. Cook, tossing periodically, until the meat is browned, approximately 3 minutes. Remove the steak from the skillet using a slotted spoon and set it aside.
6. Add the bell pepper and onion and mix well. Cook, stirring periodically, for approximately 5 minutes, or until they begin to brown.
7. Cook, stirring regularly, for 30 seconds after adding the garlic.
8. Return the meat to the pan, along with any liquids that have gathered, and the cauliflower. Combine the lime juice and chilli powder in a mixing bowl. Cook, stirring constantly, for 2 to 3 minutes, or until everything is well warmed.

Nutrition:

- 310 calories
- Fat: 18 g
- Protein content: 27 g
- 13 g carbohydrate
- 2 g of sugar
- 3 g dietary fibre
- The sodium content is 93 mg.

Printed in Poland
by Amazon Fulfillment
Poland Sp. z o.o., Wrocław
08 December 2022

b85dfc6f-75ab-4a83-b2f1-0d93e71829caR01